FIGURES IN CHINA'S SPACE INDUSTRY

Who is Ren Xinmin?

www.royalcollins.com

FIGURES IN CHINA'S SPACE INDUSTRY

Who is Ren Xinmin?

By Ye Qiang and Dong Pingping

Books Beyond Boundaries

ROYAL COLLINS

It was the year 1945. A young man from China said goodbye to his wife and children and set off alone on the long journey to study in America. In the new country, he worked extremely hard on his schoolwork and was almost always studying, except for when he had to do part-time jobs to pay for his daily expenses. His diligence paid off, as he completed both his MA degree in Mechanical Engineering and his PhD degree in Applied Mechanics within only four years (almost half of what it usually takes for other students)! The name of this bright and hardworking young man was Ren Xinmin.

Four years later, after the founding of New China in 1949, Ren
returned to Nanjing in his home country and began to work in the
Academy of Military Science of East China Military Region. This
was the starting point of his life-long career in national defense
science and technology. There, he built his first model rocket out of
a gun barrel. When he completed the model, he was as excited as a
child with a new toy and immediately went for a test launch by the
Yangtze River.

In 1956, the great scientist of aeronautical engineering Qian Xuesen, who had also recently returned to China from America, invited Ren to join him in establishing the Fifth Academy of Ministry of National Defense (the national academy for missile development). From that time, Ren became an important pioneer in building China's space industry.

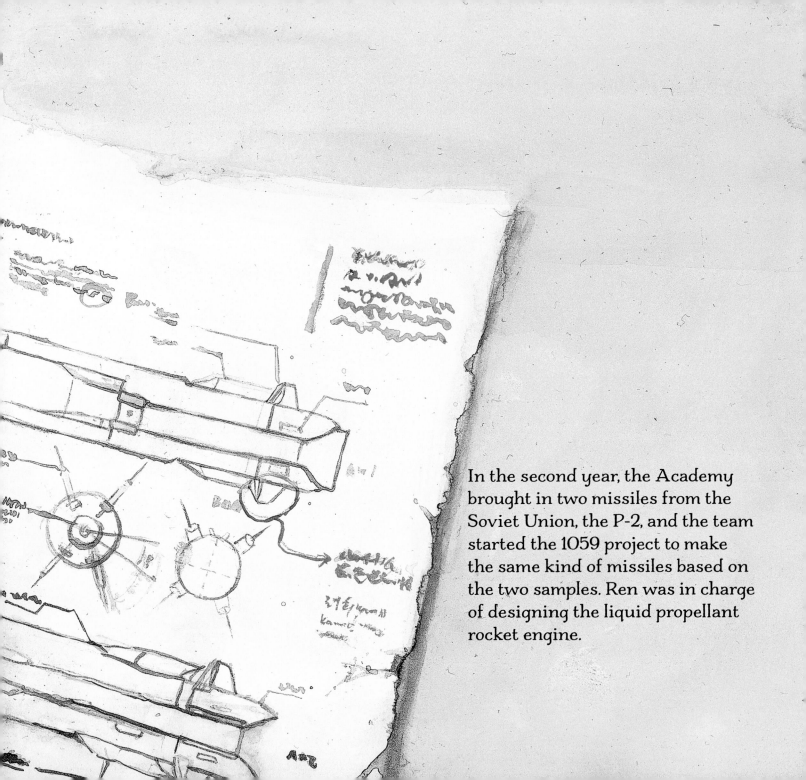

In the second year, the Academy brought in two missiles from the Soviet Union, the P-2, and the team started the 1059 project to make the same kind of missiles based on the two samples. Ren was in charge of designing the liquid propellant rocket engine.

Shocking news came out after one year's preparation work. In August 1958, translators of the P-2 missile blueprints and guidelines sent by the Soviet Union found out in astonishment that the materials were filled with mistakes. Even some critical parts such as the engine test facility were missing. But it was very difficult to get the blueprints for the test facility and the facility itself from the Soviet Union, so Ren decided to design and build a new engine test facility with all Chinese staff members. They worked day and night for three months, but the result was still not satisfactory. Ren realized that support from Soviet experts was still necessary, no matter how hard it might be. He and his team members thus contacted Nikolaj Šnjakin and other Soviet rocket scientists who were willing to help China build its own engine test facility and asked for their guidance.

But they soon lost this important support as the two countries turned from allies into enemies in 1960, and all Soviet experts had to leave China. This was greatly disappointing for Ren and his team, and it made their already challenging task of building rocket engines almost impossible. In order to overcome this hardship, Ren and his team members gave up every bit of leisure and personal life. Working and living in cold and shabby factories, they could hardly reunite with their families for three long months.

Finally, the team's first short-range liquid-propellant missile Dongfeng I successfully launched on November 5, 1960, at Jiuquan Spaceport, which marked the accomplishment of Ren's task – remaking P-2 missiles. Everyone was greatly encouraged by this achievement because they were now both equipped and experienced in building missiles; what's more, they could see their potential in developing more advanced weapons in the future.

9

Soon after the test launch of Dongfeng I, Ren was again appointed to be the Director of Engine Design for the Dongfeng II, which was going to be a completely new missile designed and made by Chinese scientists alone.

In his design, Ren made a lot of improvements to the fluid-propellant engine in Dongfeng II. Unsurprisingly, it brought new challenges to the construction, and the team experienced many setbacks and failures. But Ren didn't let these negative experiences beat him. He was always passionate about the project, and he encouraged his fellow scientists to work harder and never lose hope.

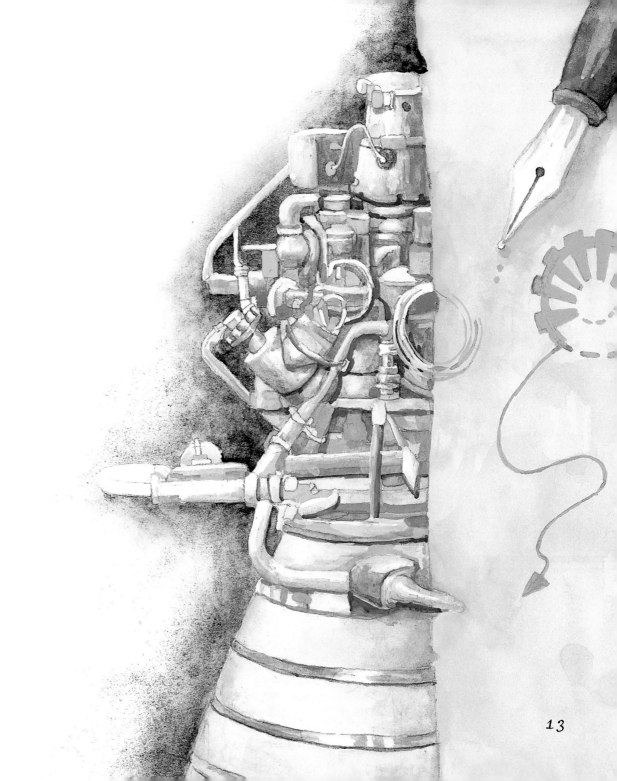

However, the long-expected test launch of Dongfeng II failed in March 1962 in Jiuquan Spaceport–a harsh blow to Ren and his team.

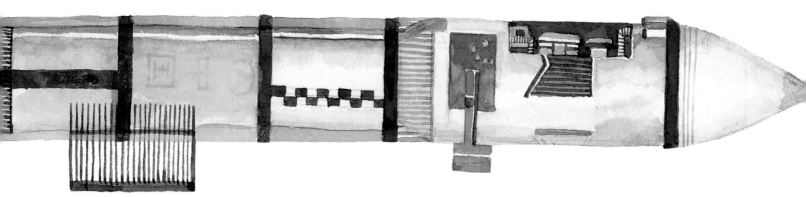

Nobody spoke at the spaceport. They were all feeling very disappointed by the failure and anxious about what might have caused the breakdown–was it the part that their group was in charge of? Then, Ren broke the silence, "People in the shock-dampener group, focus on your shock dampening; people in the quake-proof group, focus on your quake proofing. Your duties are different." Following his instructions, the team soon found out why their first test launch didn't succeed, and they quickly began to fix the problem. Two years later, on June 29, 1964, the team was ready to set up a second test launch for the updated Dongfeng II. And this time they did it! The Chinese scientists could now build their own missiles from scratch, and that was very important for a country's national defense power.

Before long, the Chinese people again welcomed the good news that Dongfeng III, which was also directed by Ren right after Dongfeng II, also succeeded in its test launch. Within only ten years, China had grown to be absolutely capable of developing its own medium-range missiles.

"We have no idea of what our father's job was back then," said Ren's eldest daughter Zhixiang in an interview. "But then we found an interesting pattern: whenever father went on a business trip, usually for several months, we knew that something huge and exciting about our country was going to happen!"

And it was true! Like the day of April 24, 1970, when the carrier rocket Changzheng I sent China's first artificial satellite Dongfanghong I into space, was definitely a historic moment for the country. The chief designer of the rocket was no other but Ren himself.

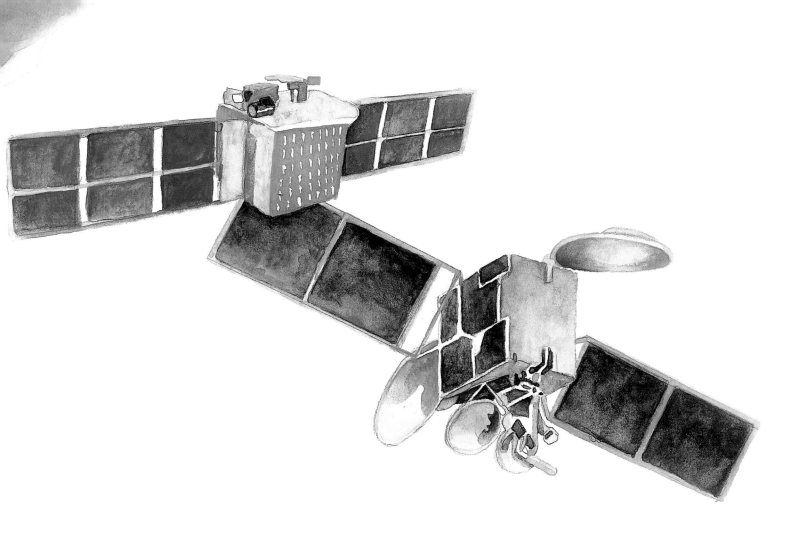

In fact, Ren had devoted almost five years of time and effort for this moment. Starting from July 1965, when he was appointed as the chief designer of Changzheng I as part of the first satellite project, he had spent numerous days and nights with his fellow scientists in factories, test centers, and labs trying to solve all kinds of difficult problems one after another while travelling to Jiuquan Spaceport again and again to test their design.

The final launch day of Changzheng I set the whole country in great excitement. It was hard for many to believe that China could have developed and sent a satellite to space independently and successfully – at that time, only four countries had ever done it!

On the evening of Labor Day (May 1) that year, members in the satellite project, including Ren and Qian (Xuesen), came to Beijing to be received by Chairman Mao Zedong and Premier Zhou Enlai at the Tiananmen Gate. They were introduced to Chairman Mao one by one. When it came to Ren's turn, Premier Zhou proudly said, "He's the one who sent the satellite up!" Hearing this, Chairman Mao marveled, "Amazing! Absolutely amazing!"

Another big project was given to Ren in June 1975. This time, he was the Vice-president of the Seventh Ministry of Machine Building, and his task was to lead the making of the carrier rocket Changzheng II and retrievable satellites – satellites that can be sent into space and brought back to earth. Within only four months, this dream turned into reality. In November, China became the third country ever to successfully launch and bring back a satellite of this kind, called the "retrievable remote sensing satellite."

Ren never felt that he had done enough in building rockets. In May 1980, he and his team surprised the world again by sending a long-range carrier rocket into the South Pacific Ocean for the first time, and it was another high-level technique in rocket science that few countries have mastered. But Ren didn't think of himself as a hero. Right after the launch, news reporters were all eager to get a word from him as the chief commander. But he was nowhere to be found in the spaceport. The truth was, Ren had already returned to where he lived, and his mind was occupied by a new space mission!

The new mission was a communication satellite. It started in 1979 when Ren was appointed to be the chief engineer for this project, which was extremely huge because it had five different systems: rocket, communication satellite, launching site, monitor and control center, and ground station. Being the chief engineer of all five systems, Ren was nicknamed the "Chief Chief Engineer," but the workload and pressure that this title brought along were not to be joked about. Experienced as he was in the field of rocket science, Ren nevertheless came across a whole new challenge: building the most advanced and powerful liquid-hydrogen-oxygen propellent rocket engine. Like every time before, when there was a difficulty, Ren and his team solved this one by repeatedly trying and testing. In May 1983, the hydrogen-oxygen engine was proven to be ready to be used on the carrier rocket Changzheng III.

At the end of the year 1983, Ren and his huge team settled in the Xichang Satellite Launch Center and began their final preparation for the launch. On January 29, the second year, the first Changzheng III carrier rocket set off. But it didn't enter its orbit as expected because the liquid hydrogen ran out, so the launch was only partly successful. Of course, Ren, as always, was not discouraged by this setback. With the help of General Zhang Aiping, he wasted no time in planning for revision and the second launch. Two months later, the second Changzheng III successfully sent the communication satellite Dongfanghong II right into its geostationary orbit on the day of April 8, 1989. At this time, China became the fifth country in the world to own her geostationary satellite in space.

Thanks to Ren's breakthroughs in building carrier rockets, geostationary satellites, and communication satellites, China ranked high in world space science development.

At the award ceremony for the founding fathers of "Two Bombs, One Satellite" in 1992, Ren received his medal of merit as an outstanding contributor to the space industry of China. The "Two Bombs" are China's first nuclear bomb and the first group of missiles. The "One Satellite" is China's first artificial satellite and geostationary satellite. A group of outstanding scientists like Ren Xinmin worked very hard for decades to make this happen, and these scientists who have devoted their whole life to the nuclear and space industry of China were awarded the "Two Bombs, One Satellite" Meritorious Medals. An extremely high honor for themselves and for all Chinese people to remember their great work! This was the year when the country's manned spaceship project was put on the table. By this time, Ren was already 77 years old, but he was still highly active in attending all the seminars related to this project. When the series of five Shenzhou spaceships were sent to space between 1999 and 2003, he was always present to witness their launches.

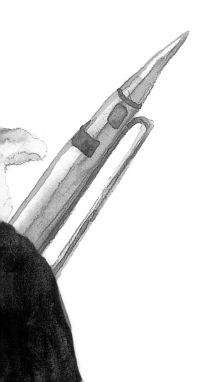

When talking about Ren and the many space projects
he has directed and participated in, people would say
that he has lived an adventurous and unusual life. But
according to Ren himself, "I've only done one thing in my
life, and that is aerospace engineering."

About the Authors

YE QIANG studied oil painting at Sichuan Fine Arts Institute. After graduating in 2001, he continued to teach in the Institute until 2008. Since then, he's been teaching as an Associate Professor in the Department of New Media Art and Design at Beihang University (Beijing University of Aeronautics and Astronautics). Ye's paintings have been displayed in hundreds of national and international exhibitions, and he has held solo exhibitions in galleries, including the Shanghai Art Museum, six times. Ye's paintings and scholarship can be found in more than 20 academic journals and monographs, such as *Art Observation*, *Art China*, *History to Chinese Oil Painting*, and more. He has also published seven textbooks, including *Basic Techniques in Drawing*, *Basic Techniques in Coloring*, and *A Brief Introduction in Abstract Painting Languages*.

DONG PINGPING is Vice-Secretary of the Party Committee and a member of the Supervisory Commission of the Department of New Media Art and Design at Beihang University.

Figures in China's Space Industry:
Who is Ren Xinmin?

Written by Ye Qiang and Dong Pingping

First published in 2022 by Royal Collins Publishing Group Inc.
Groupe Publication Royal Collins Inc.
BKM Royalcollins Publishers Private Limited

Headquarters: 550-555 boul. René-Lévesque O Montréal (Québec) H2Z1B1 Canada
India office: 805 Hemkunt House, 8th Floor, Rajendra Place, New Delhi 110 008

Original Edition © Shaanxi People's Education Press Co., Ltd.

ISBN: 978-1-4878-0890-7

To find out more about our publications, please visit www.royalcollins.com.